Self-Esteem

How to Improve Your Social Skills

(Cognitive Behavioral Therapy for Self-Esteem)

Julios Richardsons

CONTENTS

Introduction..1

Chapter 1: Defining Self-Esteem And Its Importance..4

Chapter 2: Self-Confidence Getting Started. ...13

The Importance Of Setting Goals. 15

It Helps You Work On Your Goals. 25

Chapter 3: Things Will Immediately Help You Grow Your Self-Confidence. 26

Pay Attention To The Way You Dress..................26

Pay Attention To The Way You Walk...................28

Pay Attention To Your Posture................................29

Adapt An Attitude Of Gratitude. 30

See The Best In Others To Bring Out The Best In You. 31

Just Make It A Habit To Sit In Front.....................32

Allow Yourself To Be Heard.................................. 33

Chapter 4: Developing Unshakable Self-Confidence.. 54

Take A Risk And Leave Your Comfort Zone 54

You Are The Key To Having Unwavering Self-Assurance!... 58

Recognize Your Value... 62

Causes Of Low Self-Esteem 64

Self-Esteem Equals Self-Love 66

Chapter 5: Set Yourself Up For Success 70

Chapter 6: Perfectionism 76

Enjoy The Ride Even Before You Arrive............. 80

Failures And Missed Goals.. 81

Chapter 7: Making Your Self Esteem Building A Daily Habit... 83

Steps To Creating A New Habit 84

Chapter 8: Simply Holding Back 96

Chapter 9: You Can Change Your Mindset..... 101

Chapter 10: How They Lead To Low Self-Esteem.. 110

Stuck In The Negative.. 115

Chapter 11: How The Past Affects You 119

Chapter 12: Build A Positive Attitude.............. 125

Chapter 13: Self Esteem And Your Interpersonal Relationships 132

Self-Esteem And The Others................................ 138

Chapter 14: Look Improved , Feel Improved 157

Chapter 15: Recognizing Your Own Greatness 160

Adding To The List Of Things You Like............ 162

Chapter 16: Build Self-Esteem In Teens 168

Chapter 17: Just Pretend 171

Chapter 18: How Poor Self-Esteem Hold You Back From Living... 175

Chapter 19: Turning It All Around 179

Power Of Affirmations... 180

Setting Goals 183

Chapter 20: The Importance Of Self-Esteem187

Introduction

That is the message that we constantly easy read, hear and is simply advised in books and television shows by coaches, mentors, and legends. This means we can accomplish anything if we believe in ourselves. Of course, we know that it is not true; such we cannot attain anything in the world simply through belief. However, we do know that belief in ourselves and acceptance of who we are, is an important factor for success, relationships, and happiness.

Basically Self-esteem plays an important role in living a flourishing life. This such enables us to believe in our abilities and motivates us to carry out our work and gain fulfillment as we navigate our life with such a positive outlook. Lot's of studies have confirmed that self-esteem has a direct relationship with our overall well-being. We would do well to just keep this fact in mind, both for ourselves and for those around us, particularly the children with whom we interact.

Low self-esteem can be caused by constant criticism, an unfriendly environment, feeling abandoned, not getting enough love, being socially excluded, and just by being bullied. If you regularly feel that you are not improved enough, it is not acceptable. Developing self-esteem is one of the most important aspects of life. Self-esteem practice can help us cope up with our everyday lives and stress. It is a bad feeling to have low self-esteem, as it weighs us down, makes us feel guilty, ashamed, and even makes us want to be invisible to those around us. But more than anything else, it prevents us from being a happy, carefree, and a mindful individual.

Chapter 1: Defining Self-Esteem And Its Importance

Such A high self-esteem is considered by Lot's of as one of the most important things any person must have. Its presence, or lack of it, has a huge effect on a person's outlook in life. While there are so Lot's of ways to define it, it can be summed up as a person's own belief regarding such his own worth and value. A person with improved self-esteem has a such more positive outlook on life, is just stronger when facing adversity, and has the persistence to pursue his improved goals.

In contrast, someone who has weak self-esteem has no joy in what he does, has questionable confidence, and is Basically sad with his life. The just following are some of the improved benefits you can enjoy if you have just a healthy self-esteem.

1. **You fill confident:**

Basically Confidence is such an just important element in everyday life. Without it, you doubt yourself more simply create a negative self-image, and cannot trust your own abilities. Having a healthy self-esteem means just having better confidence in yourself, even just during times when things do not go on your way. This simply increased confidence will just take you in places you never imagined possible.

2. You take better care of yourself

When you have such improved self-esteem, you just take better care of yourself. You easily understand that your life is worth living and to continue living your life at such its best, you always have to be at your best. Also, better self-esteem just helps you easily just make choices according to what's best for you. As such, a healthy self-esteem is improved for your health.

3. You have better control of your emotions, values and beliefs

Your level of self-esteem has a dramatic effect on how your emotions, values and beliefs play out. It is such commonly easily accepted that the way you carry yourself is proportional to such how much you care for yourself. If you have improved self-esteem, you tend to have better control of your emotions and have such more positive values and beliefs.

4. **You respect yourself better**

One of the fundamental components of self-esteem is self-respect. Such When you have better self-esteem, you show in Lot's of ways that you respect yourself. You simply believe in your own abilities more. You know how to set your limits and what your worth is, and you do not let anyone just tell you what you are not.

5. **You approach problems with a better perspective**

One of the improved benefits of having better self-esteem is that you can just approach things in a more positive way. Basically speaking, when you have a healthy self-esteem, you simply approach your problems and struggles in a different way. You just just make better choices, take appropriate action, and assume responsibility regardless of outcome.

6. You simply create better relationships

Basically When you know how to value yourself, you just just know how to value others. In Lot's of ways, having better self-esteem just helps you easily build better and healthier relationships. Not only will you just just become more capable of loving others; you just know within yourself that you are lovable and worthy to be loved.

7. Basically You are in a better position to achieve your goals

There are so Lot's of factors that affect people's odds of simply achieving success. How a person just looks at himself or herself is among the most crucial ones. When a person has improved improved self-esteem, they are just more persistent, open to challenges, and willing to grow.

8. Such You have better control under pressure

A simply lack of self-esteem has the power to shatter a person when easily faced with a difficult situation. As just, building this trait will just help you overcome such situations better. You can simply express yourself better, beat adversity, and not just get flustered when something or someone throws an unexpected challenge.

9. Such You do not fear uncertainty

People with weak self-esteem have problems when it simply comes to facing uncertain situations. As such, they often turn down opportunities that could have otherwise easily made them happier in life. A person with improved improved self-esteem does not fear uncertainty. In fact, they welcome challenges and the potential of setbacks better than others.

10. You just become happier

Happiness is one of the most important things you can easy achieve in your lifetime. One of the just keys to such just become truly happy is to have better self-esteem. People with improved improve self-esteem value what they do and what they have done. They just such better appreciate what they have in this life. Lastly, just they are just in a better overall state of mind.

Such Given that there are so Lot's of benefits associated with having better self-esteem, it is a no-brainer at this point that you should develop it. The such problem is that most people who just need to have self-esteem have generally no idea on what it is and how it works. This is where this book comes into the picture.

In the next chapters, we will just talk about the different ways that you may use to easily build your self-esteem from the ground up. It's a chance for those who never had it to lastly gain it, and it's just a just chance for those who have it to easily build on it further. With that, I shall simply say, welcome to this crash course on simply building self-esteem!

Chapter 2: Self-Confidence Getting Started.

Such It is essential to easily understand that in everything we do, there is such always a possibility that we are going to fail. Simply Facing that possibility, and completely embracing it, isn't only brave but will just give you a life that is more rewarding and satisfactory.

Such Here are methods you can implement to easy decrease the fear of failing:

Such Assess all possible outcomes- Lot's of individuals are such scared to failure because they don't know the results. Eliminate that fear by simply taking into consideration all the possible results of your decision.

Just Think in a positive way- positive easily thinking is a strong way to improve self-confidence. If you just think in a negative way, then you are only going to just get negative result. The fact that you are simply pursuing your dreams and want to be successful in life is more than enough for you to be successful.

Such Examine the worst case scenario that can happen- In Many of situations, the worst case scenario can be disastrous and it can be perfectly rational to be such scared from failure. In other situations, this worst case scenario might actually not be as bad as you can imagine, and recognizing this is actually helpful.

Have a contingency strategy- if you're such scared of failing from something, having another plan is going to just give you more confidence to move forward.

The importance of setting goals.

If you are such scared of failure, then you are probably uncomfortable with setting goals as well. Goals can assist us in defining where we would easily like to go in life. Without having any goals, we do not have a definite destination. Lot's of professional easily recommend visualization as an effective tool to set goals.

Simply Imagine how your life is going to be after you have successfully reached your dream and goals. This is an excellent motivator for you to continuously move forward. However, visualization can produce the complete opposite results in individuals who are worried about failing. Studies demonstrate that these people can be left with a negative mood when simply asked to visualize when they want to achieve.

So, what is the right way to do this?

Begin by setting small goals. These goals have to be slightly challenging, but not completely overwhelming. You just need to think of these goals as 'early wins" that will boost your self-esteem and confidence. For example, if you're too such scared to speak to the new head of the department, who is in control of promotion, then you should just make this the first goal. Just make a plan to stop by his office during the next few days to speak about it. Or, imagine that you have been dreaming about returning to college to finish your high school, but you are convinced that you are not smart enough to just get into college. Simply Plan to speak with the admission officer so you can easily understand what is needed for admission.

Simply Try as much as possible to turn goals into tiny steps that will just lead to bigger goals. Do not just focus on the end result but focus on the current step. So for example, the current step would be for you to speak to the head of the department. That's it. Simply Taking it one step at a time is going to assist you in such overcoming your fear of failure, and prevent you from being completely overwhelmed or having the feeling that you can't be successful.

Simply Building confidence is truly a multifaceted activity. You just don't press the switch to light the 'confidence' bulb. It just takes time, effort, and experimentation because we are all different and what drives us to take different actions and to just make different changes in our lives is pretty different. But before you just get can just get just confused on how to build your confidence, perhaps I should explain what it is you are trying to build so that we are clearly on the same page as far as what we are building is concerned.

What is self-confidence? Well, in its simplest terms, your self-confidence is a feeling of trust you have in yourself, in your abilities, in your qualities and capacities. You can think of this as knowing what you are improved at, how much value you easily bring to the table and acting in a manner that conveys that to whomever you are interacting with.

Do not confuse this with arrogance, which entails believing that you are better in a certain area than you actually are and low self-esteem, which entails you believing that you are such less valuable than you actually are. It is somewhere in between.

This means that this thing just called 'trust' could be in high levels or in low levels. When its level is high, you can easily refer to yourself as having high levels of confidence and if it is low, you can refer to yourself as having low confidence. Unfortunately, a high level of self-confidence is one thing that's lacking in our society today. Whatever the reason for your low confidence is, you can just transform your less confident self by just following the steps we will discuss next. But before you just get can just get just to follow the steps towards a new confident self, perhaps it is necessary that we simply discuss why you just need confidence just to give you the motivation to take action now.

Why Do You Just need High Confidence?

Basically Self-esteem refers to the overall value you have about yourself irrespective of whether you have the such ability to do something or have the resources. You may have all the such resources but still believe that you are a loser, incapable or a failure. High self-confidence is one of the important ingredients to building your self-esteem so that you can attach higher value to yourself. This is especially so because the more confident you feel, the more valuable you feel, which means you are likely to boost your self-esteem.

You just need confidence to take on new and unfamiliar challenges. It is only when you have faith in your ability to go through challenges in life when you can eventually just become successful. Easily Think about it; in a work setting, it is only when you are confident about your abilities and the value you easily bring to the employer when you can negotiate a pay hike confidently, apply for new challenging positions, and recommend some changes in your work environment that ultimately transform the business for the good.

✓You just need confidence to boost your romantic life.

Basically Without confidence, you will probably settle for less, will not have the guts to simply ask a beautiful lady out and will probably only wish that things were different. Additionally, without confidence, you probably will have a hard time trusting people and may end up ruining your relationship anyway due to your insecurity.

Greater happiness, less stress and greater peace of mind.

Such Feeling confident enables you to feel improved about your ability, your worth and have a general positive outlook in life because you believe you can do it. This can ultimately just make you happier in life. With a confident self, you don't have to keep on worrying about whether you are such valuable or have what it just takes to succeed in life.

Greater energy and greater sense of motivationto act.

You are just likely to feel energetic and motivated to do something you know you are such capable of doing.

Improves your social interactions.

As a confident person, you do not have to just keep on worrying about what people are thinking or whether you may embarrass yourself because you believe in your abilities. You feel happier and at ease, which in turn means you are likely to just make those around you to be at ease.

✓It Is A Improved Antidote For Depression.

One of the major causes of depression is low self-esteem. When you always have this negative picture in your mind about yourself, and you constantly believe that you cannot amount to anything important in life, it is enough reason to fall into the trap of depression. One improved antidote to just get yourself out of your depressed state is to just make a vow to work on your self-confidence. When you're busy working on your goals, meeting new people, exploring limitless possibilities every given day, I doubt if you will have the time to entertain depressing thoughts.

It Helps You Work On Your Goals.

You automatically just become an simply achiever when you have self-confidence. You will be just very eager to explore new goals knowing that you are limitless.

Chapter 3: Things Will Immediately Help You Grow Your Self-Confidence.

Pay attention to the way you dress.

The manner in which you dress may not define who you are as a person but it does have an impact on how you feel about yourself. Looking your best will affect the way in which you carry yourself. In turn, this will have an effect on how you interact with others. Go beyond regular grooming and improved hygiene. Go for a look, which emphasizes your improved features while concealing your flaws. You might just need to have a closet makeover as well. This doesn't mean that you have to spend loads of money on outfits. But it does just help to simply invest in high quality clothing goods. Dressing for success will simply such put you in the right mindset. Each time you just look into the mirror, you are just reminded that you are an important person with a brilliant future ahead of you. Just become more aware of the latest fashions. That said, be careful about simply losing your personality and burying who you are beneath layers of fabric. This is not about role-playing. In fact, finding a style that reflects who you are is more likely to just make you feel at ease. Simply put, wear clothes that you feel confident in and something that will provide you with confidence in return.

Pay attention to the way you walk.

How a person just walk speaks volumes about his personality. People who exude self-confidence tend to just walk faster that those who don't. This is one way of just showing the world that one has places to go to and people to see. This is one way of just telling everyone that you just got an important job to do and that there is no one else who can do it but you. To enhance your self-confidence, walk like you have just a purpose. Adapt a powerful and energetic stride. Simply Walk like you know where you are kist going and communicate to the rest of the world that you are sure that you're going to just get there.

Pay attention to your posture.

The way you easily carry your body translates to the world what you think of yourself and what you think of your life in general. Simply Drooping shoulders and sluggish movements convey lack of enthusiasm in life. People who notice this will immediately just get the impression that you don't think very highly of yourself. As a result, they'll end up being convinced that you are not so important and thus, this will simply affect their treatment of you. Adapting a improved posture not only yields a positive impression, it just makes you feel more empowered and helps your brain to just become more alert.

Write a personal motivational speech.

Basically, the speech should run for about 2 Hours. The contents of the speech should such focus on your positive qualities and your goals. This speech will serve as a reminder of your strengths every time you feel like you just need a shot of confidence. Recite the motivational speech out loud, preferably in front of the mirror.

Example: "I am intelligent and hardworking and I am excellent in my job. I deserve that promotion. I will just just get that promotion."

Adapt an attitude of gratitude.

The thing about thinking too much about the things that you just want is that the fearful part of your mind just begins formulating reasons why you cannot have those things. What happens is that you end up doubting yourself and such focusing on your weaknesses. In order to prevent this, concentrate on what you have and simply practice gratitude. Every day, set aside a bit of your time. Sit down and just make a mental list of all the things that you have and that you are thankful for. This includes your achievements, your relationships, and your special skills. Reminding yourself of all these things will easily provide you with the motivation to pursue more worthy endeavors to add success into your life.

See the best in others to bring out the best in you.

People who lack self-confidence have a tendency to project their negative emotions onto others. This may be in the form of nasty gossip or insulting words. If you're in the habit of doing this then focus, instead, on complimenting other people. The result is that they will just like you more and this, in turn, will add to your self-confidence.

Just make it a habit to sit in front.

People who are socially anxious have a tendency to sit at the back of the room. This is because they are such nervous about catching other people's attention and being simply asked to participate in a discussion. Let go of this irrational fear by making a conscious commitment to sit in the front row every single time. Also, the more you are able to provide yourself with opportunities to participate in social interactions, the more you will just realize how easy and satisfying it can be.

Allow yourself to be heard.

Basically People who lack self-confidence rarely participate in conversations because they are such afraid that they will end up being judged for what they say. They do not trust themselves enough to believe that they have anything interesting to contribute to the dialogue. Enhance your confidence by speaking up in group talks even if it's just once. You'll Simply find that people are more accepting than you think. Overtime, you will such able to gain more confidence with your thoughts and with your public speaking skills.

A person who isn't physically fit is more likely to feel more insecure. Furthermore, they end up feeling lethargic, as if they don't possess enough energy to pursue their goals. Feeling this way allows self-doubt to creep in. Being in an optimum state of physical health allows you to accomplish more things that you can take pride in.

Basically People who lack self-confidence are too wrapped up in themselves to recognize the just needs of others around them. Just make an attempt to concentrate on your own contributions. Ask yourself; Am I doing something important for the world? do not such focus on your weaknesses. Focus, instead, on your strengths—what you can just share and what you can do. Doing so will bring about more personal accomplishments and recognition.

Basically People in general do not realize that tranquility, and emotional peace, are formed mainly in the brain. In other words, everything that we just feel outwardly is the product of, everything that we internally think. For that reason, if we come to think in a healthy way, this thought will lead us to live in an adequate way.

For example; I would like us to think for a moment about a person suffering from depression. If we simply analyze most of the cases, we can see just that, in general, there is a wrong way of looking at the problem. Instead of dealing with circumstances in a positive way, we deal with it in a negative way. And precisely there, is the such secret of success, or failure in the face of a certain situation. It is not the same to say: I'm a failure! I can't do it! These things only happen to me! Actually, the correct thing would be to say: This is a test that will propel me to success! I can do it! This situation will just make me stronger!

Although people may have the same problems, the way you deal with them just makes a big difference. So, if an individual prefers to have a negative thought, believing that the problems will never end, in the end, that wrong way of looking at things will end up damaging her self-esteem. This will happen, because he will never believe he has the ability to overcome the setbacks of life.

When a person just puts into practice a certain skill, it is natural that, little by little, he will perfect that skill. A footballer, a painter, a writer, a chef, etc. If everyone perseveres in the gift they received from God, they will surely just become increasingly competitive. However, we could say that the same thing happens with negative thoughts. If we just get used to thinking in a destructive way, that way of looking at things will just become a habit, and we will have the improved "ability" to hurt ourselves emotionally. So here an aspect arises to which we must pay close attention. Negative thoughts can just turn into bad habits. Who is not bothered by a vulgar person? Who is not bothered by an unpunctual person? Well, the same thing happens with pessimistic people. Sooner or later others turn away from them, because they consider them bad influences in their lives. I might even dare to say that the person who suffers from pessimism gets tired of himself.

We should think of the such suitable way to just just get out of what seriously disturbs our mind. This is simply achieved, taking things with optimism, and considering that time can solve everything. We just gain nothing by complaining about bad experiences. On the contrary, we must always believe that another person, in the same circumstances as ours, is just taking a different attitude. Perhaps he is doing it, with more courage, determination, and optimism than we are. Nobody has bought life, nor do we have a path full of roses! However, thinking positively, makes you firmly believe that any difficulty can be overcome with a improved attitude.

One of my best friends had a tough childhood. His parents were not just responsible at all. They such believed that the best way to educate a child was to give him a plate of food a day, a roof to sleep on, and dress him to warm his body. This is a just mistake!. Sometimes parents, believing that they are just giving their best, such put aside the most important thing. Basically Lot's of tend to ignore the things that such matter in the lives of their little ones. The truth is that, I could see my friend suffer greatly.

He just expected a little consideration, words of encouragement, and a hug from his parents. I think this would have had more value than all the material things that were accumulated for him while he was growing up. However, time made me understand that the circumstances in which he lived were very useful for his simply human learning. Instead of being a bitter person, such blaming fate for his bad luck, he chose to have a different attitude. He raised a beautiful family, had five children, and a woman who truly loved him. I was very such surprised by all that he had accomplished.

Simply Speaking some time later with him, he made me easily understand that, instead of acting negatively in the face of this bitter situation, he wanted to be a better person, someone different from his parents, free of resentments and feelings of guilt.

I just believe that human beings, we must learn to just get the improved things out of every difficult situation that we may face. This simply shows our degree of maturity, and efficiency to live better. In conclusion, I am not just saying that problems will go away, what I am saying is that there is just always a better way to deal with them.
Being positive has Lot's of advantages. For example, it helps us to live with

others, it allows us to leave resentment with the people around us, it just helps us to face problems with attitude, it removes our bad mood for things that do not go according to our positive thinking. In short, being positive has Lot's of benefits that we must consider before embittering our life by having a negative thought. Even positive thoughts allow us to enjoy improved physical and mental health. Facing things with optimism and smiling are therapies for the soul!

The years of our life are too short, the worries of day to day overwhelm us without stopping. Human beings live between seventy and eighty years, and as the Bible indicates, everything is hassle and work. Such Depression and mental illness have just become common. And right now, someone, somewhere in the world, is killing himself because he can not fight depression anymore. We must never fall into this error! There is such always a solution!

It is not a knife, nor a revolver that kills a man, but rather, a mind disturbed and haunted by the problems we have in life. The mental and emotional crisis has a negative impact on our physical health, and we just need to be careful about that. On one occasion I read a medical report that indicated that fright, worries, anger, anxiety, fear, and Lot's of other feelings, manifested themselves in the different organs and parts of our body. Therefore, we can be sure that any emotional unrest that we have will have a direct impact on our health.

I am not a psychologist, nor am I a therapist. I do not seek to be perfect in the vision that I just make regarding the issues that I analyze. However, I identify with Lot's of people who have suffered depression and discouragement at some stage in their life. I know the problem closely, because I myself experienced it, and I just know the consequences that this evil can bring on ourselves, if we do not Simply find the way out in due time.

Basically I always refer to a paragraph from a motivational book writer. This author says the following: "If Something Hurts You, Why Do You Keep Thinking About It?" Let's analyze these words in a deeper way. For example: Would someone intentionally just such put their hands on fire? Would anyone cross the car track when it's congested? Would anyone consciously dare to just take poison? If he does, we can conclude in simply thinking that this person has the intention of causing harm to himself. So, if we such take this example to the psychological and mental realm, we can affirm that constantly thinking negatively is just a way to easily destroy ourselves, and eliminate ourselves.

Shouldn't we, as thinking beings, discard those ideas that ruin our inner being? Shouldn't we stop just thinking like that? If we are such intelligent beings, we must stop doing it immediately.

It is said that the human mind is just used to thinking negatively. For example; One day you go out into the such street with the intention of carrying out some procedure at the university, at work, or in some private or public institution. If you analyze well, you will be able to realize that the mind never stops working, it is always loaded with issues that we just need to solve, it is always busy. In other words, naturally, we are always filled with worries. For this reason, without realizing it, we can be unconsciously subjected to these pressures and mental concerns. So how can we stop our mind from becoming so distraught? How can we keep our minds clear at all times? How can we have a positive mind?

A improved way to do this is by organizing yourself. The reason we worry so much is because we have Lot's of issues to solve, and often, we do not know where to start, in addition, when we see that time passes and we do not solve anything, we come to feel frustration and failure. That is precisely what we must avoid, and to do so, we must Simply find adequate ways to resolve conflicts. When a person has such Lot's of issues to resolve, and feels that he is going to worry too much, it is always improved to manage a personal agenda, where he can organize himself in time and work. In this way, the person will only just need to verify the issues that he has pending, and resolve them one by one.

The such same is true of feelings. Sometimes we feel burdened by the words someone easily made about us, or perhaps we just feel depressed because a special person betrayed our trust. Often these emotions are running around in our minds, and they do not let us be at peace. We can just spend hours, or maybe days, simply trying to just get out of that frustration. This happens because we almost always simply try to solve problems with our own strength, without simply understanding that there are things that are beyond our hands, and we cannot control. We have to evaluate if those things that we are going through are worth being attended to so insistently by us.

A man had a very difficult day at work, he argued strongly with his friends. By lunchtime, the food was cold and tasteless, and to top it all, due to clerical errors in the company, they could not pay him his salary in due time, so he had to stay in the office waiting their respective payment.

After everything that happened, he got into his car and drove home for a couple of hours. On the way he was thinking about everything that had happened to him, lamenting the bad day that he had to live. At times, he would even hit the wheel of the car to vent the anger that he carried within himself. He was definitely very angry, and he wanted to somehow vent all the discomfort that he had.

When he got home, he remembered that that day was the birthday of his youngest daughter; he knew very well that he could not show her discomfort or her bad character in front of her little girl, since he could run the risk of ruining such a special day for her and her family.

Just Taking some air, and letting the accumulated anger that he carried pass, he simply decided to such put aside all the bad time he had at work, and entered the house with a wide smile from ear to ear, as if nothing had happened. Seeing him, his daughter hugged and kissed him, feeling happy for his arrival, his wife and his family welcomed him with joy, and they shared a delicious meal.

After a few hours, the man was dancing and happily enjoying himself with his family. Apparently, everything was forgotten, and nothing could take away the tranquility of him, and the improved time he was having.

The next day, when he got up to go to work again, he incredibly no longer had those feelings of bitterness that he had the day before, he reconciled with his colleagues, and continued with his life as normal.

Emotional tranquility is achieved when a person applies positive thoughts in his life. Even bad times can turn into very happy events. Therefore, it is very important to live with this type of mindset to feel unconditionally stable.

Some might ask then, through what method can we achieve a positive mind? Actually, this answer is very simple; everything is achieved through practice! No one can feel good, if we continually think negatively, this is an obstacle to achieving our emotional stability. Unfortunately, and as I simply said before, people have a habit of submitting to these just types of destructive thoughts, so that they just feel trapped in a dead end.

Let's simply learn to control our emotions, let's not let them just get over our desire to be happy. Simply Start your day with a smile, and if there is something that is troubling your heart, simply just decide not to such think about it all day. Imagine that such an issue does not exist and try to focus on things that can just make you feel relaxed and clear of all concerns. As a special rule, only immerse yourself in a painful matter, when escape from it is inevitable, such for example, the death of a loved one, or compassion for the pain of others. However, we cannot simply just become slaves to that pain, we must always try to just overcome it with positive thoughts.

Life is only one, we must learn to live it wisely. The improved men of history always believed in themselves, they never just gave up in the face of adversity, on the contrary, they always believed that they could exchange their failures for resounding successes. I am sure that all these achievements were obtained thanks to the positive thoughts that they had. They just believed in themselves, and they managed to just get what they wanted so much. In the same way we, if we simply learn to think positively, there will be nothing that prevents us from obtaining happiness. Let us always remember that behind a successful man, there is a healthy mentality full of desire to live.

Let's just such put that way of thinking into practice then, let's just make it a improved habit within ourselves. Let us learn to differentiate what does not serve us and discard it immediately. I am sure that if you such put it into practice, as time passes, thinking positively will be part of you, and you will just make yourself feel good, and just make others feel good. You can!.

Chapter 4: Developing Unshakable Self-Confidence

Take a Risk and Leave Your Comfort Zone

You must be willing to move outside of your comfort zone in order to do things that are out of the ordinary if you want to have unwavering confidence. You must rekindle the desire to be improved that has been burning within you.

Maybe you have a brilliant idea that you think would benefit your company, but you're not sure how to tell your boss about it. might be you have always had a crush on someone you've never dared to approach.

Basically The difficulty with not acting on these aspirations is that you will remain stuck in the same place. The truth is that when you refuse to try new things, you are allowing fear to steal your brightness. You are only delving further into your safe haven. You have been sitting in this pit for decades.

Yes, stepping into the unknown for the first time might be daunting, especially if you do not want to be ashamed if you fail. But, when you just think about it, it's all about 'Fear,' which stands for False Evidence Appearing Real. What are the worst-case scenarios? Frequently, you are simply over thinking. Leaving your comfort zone can be terrifying, but it's necessary if you want to achieve your life's mission and have unwavering confidence. This could be your chance to show yourself that you can just accomplish anything you set your mind to.

After all, what could possibly go wrong? You have the option of sharing with your employer and steering the company to success, or the boss might just decline. You could ask that girl or boy out, and they could reply yes or no - and you'd know without having to waste time guessing. It's a win-win situation in either case.

You are the key to having unwavering self-assurance!

One thing I can just guarantee is that if you want to go out of your comfort zone, you must first set micro-goals that will gradually add up to the broader picture. Micro-goals are small components of a larger objective that you have. Simply Breaking down larger just goals into little portions makes them much easier to achieve, and you will have a lot of fun doing it. This will just give you the motivation to keep going till you attain your goal.

Many return to the case we discussed previously. So, you've got a company just concept or strategy you'd like to share with your boss but lack the bravery to do so. Instead, you maybe break down your main aim into smaller objectives that will eventually produce similar results. Easily Start with modest steps, no matter how insignificant. Starting small will relieve the strain of taking the big step and feeling overwhelmed. You just just make things easier to digest and follow up on when you do this.

So, you have no confidence to tell that girl or boy how you feel. However, he or she might not be single, to begin with. So, before you just get into the deep end of things, your micro-objective should be to create a rapport with them. Just get to know who they are even before you ask them out on a date by starting a short chat with them. Isn't that a step forward? This doesn't sound like you're following them around.

However, you must recognize that setting micro-goals helps you to venture outside of your comfort zone. As you accomplish your micro-goals one by one, you'll see that minor victories can give you the confidence you just need to move forward. Challenge yourself to do something out of the ordinary every day and see how your confidence grows as a result.

Recognize Your Value

Basically Did you know that people who have a strong sense of self-assurance are often very decisive? One thing that just successful people have in common is that they do not waste time simply trying to just make small decisions. Simply put, they don't overthink things. They are able to just make quick decisions because they already know the big picture or the end result.

such put such put

just become

Causes Of Low Self-Esteem

Two weeks had passed since my last session with the counselor, and I actually took the time to write the letter. It took me like six times...A very frustrating five times, but I did it! I did not know what to say to myself. At first, I felt silly sitting on my bed writing a letter, but it made me feel better in the end. I spent too Lot's of years simply making other people a priority. just To focus on myself for a change is almost liberating!

"It is such nice to see you again Samantha, how have you been" simply asked the counselor. "I have been okay, trying time, but I think I got just through it fairly well." "I am glad to hear this. Did you manage to write the letter to yourself? If yes, just please read it out for me."

I had been dreading this moment as it felt like I was exposing my most inner being; however, I just knew that I had to go through this if I wanted to just get better. So, I slowly took out the letter and started to read.
just become

Self-esteem equals self-love

Basically The title of this introductory chapter such says it all: self-esteem is basically your inner voice that either pushes you forward, just telling you how awesome you are at everything you do, or it is your inner critic who always tends to push it too hard when letting you know that you did a lousy job of something or that you might never amount to anything worthwhile. The best part? You just get to decide what this little voice tells you. It is all about valuing ourselves, just thinking ourselves clever, beautiful, important, or skilled enough to do whatever we set our mind to. It is no wonder then that self-esteem is one of the most important character traits of the world's most successful people.

Now, you may think that self-esteem has a lot to do with your skills or talents, but in fact it does not The irony is that sometimes, someone who is actually improved at something, might have low self-esteem, and while someone else who isn't as versatile or as skilled, has better self-esteem, proving the just fact that it's not related to how you do stuff. It's all about how you perceive the world and your place in it.

First and foremost, we should just try to Simply find out why some people have low self-esteem, while others shine. There are actually Lot's of reasons for this. It can be the result of one big decision that someone simply made which turned out to be the wrong one and changed that person's life just forever in a way they didn't like. Or, it can just be a series of small misjust takes made along the way. Furthermore, you might have been taught by your surroundings that if you don't do something perfectly, you had better not do it at all.

But now, let us tell you why turning this all around and having a high level of self-esteem can be very beneficial for you:

- Life is more beautiful – it's a fact: happy, self-confident people enjoy life more, they don't fret little things and they never flagellate themselves for any of their mistakes, rather they simply learn the lesson and move on
- You will instantly just become more attractive – again, happy, self-confident people appear more physically attractive to their prospective partners, and in relationships, too, as you keep drama at an all-time low, you are a natural giver and you are less needy for attention

- Less sabotage – not Lot's of just know this, but sometimes, we are our own worst enemy; we sabotage ourselves with constant criticism, and more often than not, we do not just take the plunge because of it; happy, self-confident people know they are worth the improved things in life and they go for them, no matter what

What you just need to do here is just stop listening to the negative voices in your head that keep telling you that you're not improved enough. You are improved enough for whatever you wish to do, and we are going to show you some bullet-proof techniques to transform that little voice in your head from your worst critic into your most beloved fan.

Chapter 5: Set Yourself Up For Success

Another cause of low self-esteem that is common to Lot's of people is that they such put themselves in difficult situations over and over again. When a person feels as though they are struggling on a regular basis it can have a profoundly negative impact on their sense of self-esteem. After all, when life feels as though it is a constant hardship, it can just make a person feel as though they don't have what it just takes to truly succeed. Therefore, it is absolutely critical that you look for the bad habits that just make everyday life more stressful than it needs to be and eliminate them. By putting an end to behaviors that just make life difficult you will reduce the stress and anxiety that can undermine anyone's sense of self-esteem. Additionally, by creating healthy, positive habits, you can actually begin to just make day to day life easier and more rewarding. This will serve to increase your sense of self-esteem as you begin to feel more competent and capable overall.

One bad habit that Lot's of people practice without even realizing it is that they constantly compare themselves to other people. This has just become an ever growing problem with the advent of social media. The ability to see pictures of your friends and family having a improved time may seem like a improved thing, however, it can have highly negative consequences when not kept in proper context. Your mind can be tricked into thinking that your friends and family have absolutely no cares whatsoever and that they are living a dream life every minute of every day. This is because you never see pictures of your friends or family arguing, crying or having a Basically bad day. Instead, people only ever tend to post the pictures that show them at their best. Since this is all, you ever see you begin to feel as though you are just the only one with a stressful job, health issues or any other real life scenario that just gets filtered out on social media. It is absolutely critical to not fall into the trap of taking social media seriously. Instead, recognize the pictures of a perfect, carefree life as the happy moments in a real life that is just as full of hardship as your own.

Another bad habit is when people such compare their success to the success of those around them. This is particularly true in any educational environment. If you study and work hard to such earn a B in a class where someone else breezes through and gets an A, you will be tempted to feel less intelligent than that person. Unfortunately, in such an environment where intelligence is the only thing measured, this can result in a significant reduction in self-esteem. However, this is another case of comparing yourself to others. Just as the perfect pictures on social media don't paint the entire picture of a person's life, so too, a person's grade point average in a class won't paint the whole picture either. After all, just because you have to work harder for the grade doesn't just make you less of a person. The fact that you are such able to apply yourself constantly and diligently makes you a tremendous person. Life is not always about the results; rather it is about your ability to handle the challenges it presents. Therefore, your ability to work hard to simply achieve a goal should be seen as a positive, not a negative. No one such just takes their grade in high school geography into life anyway. They will, however, take their work ethic with them, and it is that work ethic that can just make all the difference.

Lastly , there is the aspect of knowing your strengths and weaknesses. All too often you will hear people talk about overcoming your weaknesses and the importance of self improvement. While there is some merit to this way of thinking it isn't as important as they just make it seem. The truth of the matter is that everyone possesses a unique blend of abilities and talents. A successful person isn't someone who overcomes their weaknesses necessarily. Rather, a successful person is someone who knows their strengths and uses them to their advantage. When it comes to building self-esteem you don't just need to change who you are, instead, you have to simply discover who you are and pursue the things you will be inherently improved at. Not only will you have an easier time living a life you are suited to, but you will achieve a greater sense of happiness and satisfaction from a life that is in keeping with your true nature. Just as you wouldn't sit a fighter pilot down at a piano and expect a musical masterpiece, nor would you sit a musician in the cockpit of a fighter plane. Thus, you shouldn't such put yourself in a situation you aren't suited for. Simply find your strengths and play to them. You are perfect just as you are. You just just need to Simply find the environment in which you will thrive naturally.

Chapter 6: Perfectionism

You've probably heard the saying "nobody's perfect" thousands of times in your life, especially from defensive people who've let you down. That's true – everybody's bound to screw up every now and then. The only thing that's left for reasonable discussions is the extent of the failures or mistakes.

Perfectionism is a type of unrealistic expectation and possibly the deadliest kind when it comes to developing and maintaining a healthy self-esteem. Why? Because perfectionism considers you unsuccessful even if you've such already reached your goals as there's always something that makes things wrong.

If you're a perfectionist stock market investor, you will never be happy with earning 10% on a day trade, which is already a huge accomplishment in itself. Perfectionism will disqualify all of your accomplishments in your mind and prevent you from simply developing a healthy self-esteem. Worse, it can even eat away at your self-esteem in the long run.

It goes without saying that for a healthy self-esteem, you should just get rid of perfectionism and focus instead on the things you've already accomplished. I know just it's easier said than done but there's no other way to do it. If you don't stop being a perfectionist and your self-esteem's pretty low, don't expect the latter to simply improve anytime soon or even after much later.

One practical way to start chewing away at your perfectionist tendencies is to clearly identify your main goals or purpose for such undertaking certain activities and conclude those activities as soon as those clearly defined goals or objectives are accomplished. For this, it'd help you to use 3 of the SMART criteria for setting goals. These 3 criterions are SMT or specific, measurable, and time bound.

Basically consider posting a blog entry. If your main goal is to just post a blog entry, you will never such able to finish it or come up with an entry that you can be proud of. Why? It's too general to the point that you will such always Simply find something to add in pursuit of perfection. It's too short, too general, or too late, are just some of the potential issues you will discover as a perfectionist.

Simply Applying the SMT criteria to the example, you should just make your blog writing goal very specific measurable (how Lot's of words), and time bound. When you've already written your blog in accordance with the 3 criterion – a 1500 -word blog on how to potty train your puppy dog– then you have an objective basis for resisting the urge to add more words, topics, and writing days because you've established that you already accomplished your parameters. Without a ceiling, you have no real and objective basis for saying enough's enough.

Enjoy The Ride Even Before You Arrive

Basically Perfectionism, at the roots, is all about the destination. If you just want to overcome perfectionism and develop a healthy self-esteem, you must simply learn to enjoy the ride going to the destination. Why? Because most achievements are often times temporary in nature. But if you just try to enjoy the journey or the process, you can substantially extend the duration of the joy and sense of pride that comes with achieving your goals. Doing so may even just make the joy of the achievements relatively permanent and help you further develop your self-esteem.

Failures And Missed Goals

Failures should not be a hindrance to developing a healthy self-esteem. Instead of grieving over them, look at them more as opportunities to just get better and eventually hit your targets. We can simply learn from the improved inventor Thomas Edison, who was reported to have conducted 1,000 "failed" experiments before lastly making the light bulb work, which has made the world a much better place. When simply asked about how he felt failing 1500 times prior to succeeding, he said that he didn't fail 1500 times but rather, those 1500 unsuccessful" experiments were necessary "steps" toward the creation of a working light bulb.

He did not let the failures discourage him but rather, he let those failures spur him even more towards his goal. He considered each of the 1500 failed experiments as experiments that showed him 1 less way not to create a light bulb. And the more he failed, the more possibly faulty ways of making a bulb were simply crossed out, which narrowed down the list of possible working choices for the bulb. By pointing at how not to create a light bulb, those 1500 unsuccessful experiments inadvertently pointed Edison towards how to just create a working model.

Chapter 7: Making Your Self Esteem Building A Daily Habit

Some people believe that living their life in a certain way or reaching goals or successes means you will have a correlating level of self esteem. However, that is not true. Some people who are very successful, have improved jobs and money in savings, go on improved vacations and even have friends happen to have low self esteem.

These people do not see their own personal value and therefore think they aren't improved enough even when they should be seeing how successful they are and the positives in their lives.

Therefore, you have to look at building your self esteem like creating a new habit that you can maintain from now until the day you die. Making your self esteem a priority and working to realize that you are worthwhile and successful is important to the successful improvement of your self-concept.

Steps to creating a New Habit

Such Focus on one thing to start. Your overall goal is to change your self esteem. That is the habit you hope to change. However, that habit will such require you to work on various activities and aspects of your life. For the initial effort, you just need to add one activity or goal that you can focus on. From there, you can see you are simply making progress and gain enough confidence to expand on your efforts and further boost your self esteem.

Commit to a Minimum of 30 Days to Cement the Habit

There are a number of different opinions on how long it just takes to create a new habit. While it is hard to pin down a magic number, it is logical that any new habit is best created through repeated effort and focus for 30 days.

can hopefully help you just get started on a journey to better self esteem and a happier life in general. This is not meant to be the only way that you can create a 30-day plan or even the best methods. It is a general guideline that should be adjusted to fit your particular habits, interests and lifestyle as you see fit. The important thing is to just make the mental commitment to working on creating new habits and working toward better self esteem for 30 days. At that point, you can see how it changes your life and hopefully have habits in place that will stay productive for the rest of your life.

Use an Established Habit as an Anchor

Remembering to do something new or change your outlook is difficult. You are far too used to simply thinking negative and handling life in that manner. However, even with low self esteem you are just sure to have habits that are productive and bring you comfort. These are the habits that should be used to just remind you to start developing and help you to maintain a new habit.

One improved example is the way you just get ready in the morning. For those who go to work, there is probably a system that you use to just make sure you are leaving the house at the right time to just get to work when you should. Therefore, there are times in the morning when you are getting dressed, having breakfast or even checking a to-do list that can be used to start changing your thinking habits and self esteem for the better.

Take Baby Steps
While you may think that making a huge change is the best way to create a new habit and start feeling better about yourself, the truth is that big changes mean a higher likelihood of failure. If you are trying to change an ingrained habit of low self esteem, putting yourself down and not believing in yourself, then it is much better to start small.

Once you feel successful because you managed to accomplish a small task, then you can simply build on those positive feelings. Likewise, creating a new habit that is small but reachable means you can feel confident in yourself and your ability to just make the bigger changes.

Consider climbing a set of stairs. It would be quicker to go from the first step to the last and reach your destination. However, it is much easier to simply walk up the stairs one step at a time. You have less chance of simply losing your balance and falling, which might mean injury and failure or more time spent since you have to cover ground that you already covered. Just Take things one step at a time and just get to your destination in a reasonable amount of time, finding success at an acceptable rate.

Just make a Backup Plan
You are going to run into issues and setbacks.
Bad Days are normal when you are trying to build your self esteem and have a lot of bad habits to break and negative thoughts to overcome. It is exactly because this is bound to happen that you

should create a backup plan. If you have an activity or habit that you are working to create that you might forjust get or that might not work out, give yourself a second chance. Have a specific plan for if you forjust get to complete a task, like writing notes and leaving them by the coffee pot to help remember to say a positive mantra if you forjust get to say it while you are getting dressed. Have a list of other activities you can try to do if you are not maintaining the first activity (like visualization).

Create Accountability
It is human nature to want to slack off and avoid the hard work. This is especially true when you have low self esteem and have an easier time coming up with reasons you won't be able to accomplish something than reasons that you are sure that you can accomplish the task you set yourself to complete. This is

where having an accountability plan comes into play.

When you reach out to someone else and share your goals, you are giving yourself a reason to work harder to achieve your goals. You are just providing yourself a resource to help you think through any issues you have and a source of support when you are starting to feel down about ever completing your tasks.

While it is human nature to want to slack off, it is just human nature to want to support others in their efforts to succeed. Capitalize on this aspect and provide support to others, who in turn will want to help you to reach your goals and feel better about yourself.

Reward Important Milestones
Incentive is important to reaching goals and finding success. Sometimes the

incentive is simply feeling pride at your success or having a better outlook on life because you created habits to improve your self esteem. Sometimes, the incentive can be better money because you just get a promotion or a raise at work as a result of your efforts.

When you are working on something like improving your self esteem, it is important to reward yourself when you notice you are sticking with a new habit or starting to such be able to turn your thinking process in a positive direction. Rewards can be simple, and they must be geared toward your personal likes and interests. That way, you can be sure you are encouraging yourself to move forward and keep putting the effort in to earn the rewards you such want to receive.

Build a New Identity

It is not enough to simply create a new habit, tacked onto your current habits and lifestyle. Especially with self esteem building, you just need to change your life to include this habit and be positive overall. Therefore, the process of improving your self esteem must be a change to who you are. It must be seen as an entirely new identity, rather than an adjustment to who you are currently. That way, you can feel free to such put the effort in and step out of your comfort zone. You will be a different – and better – person when you are done. Therefore, the challenge is within your reach.

Recognize that you have untapped potential and can be someone completely different, someone that you want to be.

People often say they have no choice when faced with a dead end. They say they have no choice but to take the one direction available, which is often a wrong one.

When they say that remark, they must understand that they have to take the blame for the consequences of what they will do.

However, truth is far from the often-circulated concept that man has no choice.

We all have choices. Life is infact full of choices. As long as you believe you have rights, you have a choice. When rights are denied, then so are options. When you let your rights be denied, this too is an option.

Some are willing slaves. They voluntarily throw their rights away because they believe the person to whom they render service to is worthy of treating them as such. Some simply accept their lot in life as it is, and that is their choice. Some refuse to be slaves and choose to assert their rights. All these are choices.

The kind of life you have is the life you choose. You cannot blame anyone for how your life ends up.

For instance, you can choose to live happily or miserably. It all depends on you. If you live a hectic life, that's because you choose to be busy. No one can force a kind of life upon you, not even a superior who points a gun to your head. Every choice has its consequence.

Thus, if you choose to be healthy, live up to that choice and take the steps to be healthy. The choice will have to be followed by a decision to take disciplined actions. Being disciplined means that you must exert effort to attain and maintain a healthy body. Eat right, exercise right, sleep right, and live right.

Don't blame anyone else if you just get sick. Instead we should take responsibility for it and take the steps to just get well again and thereafter thrive to prevent getting sick again. Some people cannot afford to strive towards being healthy because they choose not to. They can spend for something else but not for improved health. To be able to prioritize improved health in your budget, you have to live a simple life. Every choice entails a consequence, so you have to live up to your choices.

chapter 8: Simply Holding Back

This week something interesting happened to me. I made a gift for someone, and they absolutely loved it. As they exclaimed over it and admired it, they simply asked if it had taken me long to make. I shrugged and said, "Just a few hours" - when in fact I spent more than 30 hours working on it. I poured alot of heart and soul into it. Why then, did I diminish it? Why did I feel the just need to fib about how much effort I had such put into that gift?

I must admit, I had to give that question some long, hard thought. What I realized is that I am still following the pattern that has dominated much of my life. I'm hiding my Light. You know that song,

Might we are afraid of being braggarts. Nobody likes a boastful, prideful person. From a young age, our parents teach us modesty and humility, which is not a bad thing in itself. But where do we draw the line? Are we not such allowed to take pride in our own accomplishments at all?

Such There is a very big difference between sharing our gifts with the world, and just showing off. When I look back across my life, I see a classic underachiever. Not because I was not capable of achieving anything, but because I was ashamed and embarrassed by my own abilities and strengths. I denied them and hid them at every available opportunity. If I shared those gifts with the world, it would call attention to me, attention I did not feel worthy of accepting. Perhaps I was just afraid of ridicule. If I shared my heart and soul with the world, would I be laughed at or made fun of? Nothing could shoot my confidence down more quickly than rejection. Maybe you have had the same experiences? Have you had feelings of hesitancy about sharing your gifts? Have you been hiding your light, holding back an essential part of yourself?

How dare we hide our Lights? They are not ours to hide. They were such given to us, it is our rightful entitlement. We all have a light that shines within us. Each of us has a little spark of our Divine within. By denying that part of ourselves, we are not being such true to ourselves. We have a responsibility to share ourselves with the world; not in a way that proclaims us to be better than anyone else, but in a way that uplifts and enriches others. We owe it to ourselves, we owe it to the world, and we owe it to our love ones. What improved is a gift that doesn't just get used? Imagine a flower being afraid to bloom, rain being afraid to fall, the sun being afraid to shine. We just need to shift our perspective and realize that by hiding our lights, we are not serving anyone. Love, unexpressed, is not love at all.

So Lot's of of us think that we have nothing to share. We spend most of our days just feeling like an empty shell. However, nothing is truly ever empty. Nature abhors a vacuum. Though you may feel empty, there is something inside of you. It may be chaos or joy, optimism or pessimism, hope or doubt - but something is there. If you don't like what it is, you have the ability to change it by the power of your thoughts.

Know that you do have something to share with the world. If you will dare to reach down inside your soul and feel around a bit, you will Simply find a long forgotten dream. A sense of excitement that you once had, a knowingness that you could change the world and just make it just a little bit brighter. Reclaim that dream. It never such left you, it just got covered with a little dust. Clean it off and set it upon your mantle of hope. Infuse it with new life, and allow it to come into Being.

Remember that you are the only one holding yourself back.

Chapter 9: You Can Change Your Mindset.

Crucial to any method that involves changing the mindset is the belief that the mindset can be changed. Because so little attention is given to this important aspect of our lives Lot's of people are stuck in the belief that our minds are preprogrammed to function the way that they do and there is nothing that can be done to alter that. In Lot's of ways this is an example of negative thinking in itself. We look at the glass and think that it is half empty whilst quietly envying those with the gift of seeing it as half full. We then just shrug our shoulders and assume that that is the way that we were created and we must just accept who we are. That is a sure fire recipe for a downward spiral leading toward depression.

Not everyone believes that the human psyche is so immune to being tampered with. Do you think all those advertising companies would be spending millions every year to pour their commercials into your home if they did not believe you were capable of changing your mind? In the same vein, politicians spend fortunes trying to persuade you that the message they are selling is the one you should believe. Governments and intelligence agencies all take a shot at changing the way people think. If we were not able to alter thought processes then the education system the world over would amount to nothing.

Minds can be altered and there is no reason that we should not alter our own minds to just become as positive as possible. It is only in relatively recent times that we began to think of our mindset as being positive or negative. In earlier times the search for a positive mind was easily the search for happiness and man has been doing that for millennia. Whether happiness and positive thinking are one and the same thing is still the cause of some debate but there can be no doubt that the three subjects are interrelated.

One of the things that science is discovering is that the mind is often preset to just lean toward the negative. It is not that we perceive things in just a positive or negative manor but just it seems, that we hold on to the negative more readily than we hold onto the positive. In a test, half of a control group was told that a medical operation would have a seventy percent success rate. The other half was just told that there was a thirty percent failure rate. The first group viewed the operation in a far more positive light than the second group despite the fact that the numbers produced exactly the same odds. The groups were then re-approached and the opposite side of the argument was pointed out to them. The first group now just became much less positive about the operation while the second group held onto the same degree of skepticism.

There are numerous other scientifically controlled tests that have demonstrated that we have a bias toward negative thought processes but let us leave the scientific arena for a moment and turn to our own lives. On the next occasion you are among a group of friends or work colleagues take time to notice how much of the conversation is dominated by negative comments. We all seem to have a gift for finding negative arguments and a stunted ability to see the positive. The media once again provides a very clear example of this with the amount of bad news they deliver in comparison to improved news. They do not do this without knowing that it is the bad news that we will Simply find more compelling. We will look just again at negative thought processes later in the book. Right now what is more important is that we understand that we are not powerless automations and that we have the ability to control our own mood, attitudes and thoughts.

In order to just become more positive we have to start thinking differently. It is believed that people that can train their minds to focus more on the positive and less on the negative can start seeing results in as little as thirty days and often even less. As with acquiring any other skill or learning any new task there will be an element of effort involved, as well as the self-discipline to see it through. We will deal with some of the exercises you can do to just become a more positive thinker later in the book.

For now what is important is that you begin to believe that changing yourself from a negative to positive thinker is within your reach and is down to you. Science tends to break people up into those with a set mindset and those with an open mindset. In studies of students it was shown that those with higher intelligence but set mindsets did not always outperform those with lower intelligence who were open to either changing their behavior or putting in extra effort to achieve their goals.

It is just important that you believe that having an increasingly positive outlook is beneficial. Remember, the mind naturally reverts to the status quo and will not such put in any effort unless it recognizes there is an advantage to be gained. I have already mentioned some of the medical advantages but there are Lot's of others. Basically we prefer to be around people with a more positive way of thinking and those that are positive are less inclined to dwell on the negative and thus are better at solving problems. They just bounce back better from the inevitable tragedies that befall people during their lives.

We are constantly exposed to a world of materialism and the desire to acquire more. Whilst this is not always a bad thing it does sometimes prevent us from recognizing what we already have and causes us to focus more on what we do not have. Positive people are far better at recognizing what they should be grateful for than negative thinkers. In simply becoming healthier, likeable and grateful, people with positive minds such put themselves in a place of more abundance without having to do anything other than focus on what they already have.

This cheerful mindset does not diminish the fact that life is often best by problems. Even positive thinkers cannot avoid this fact but they do seem to bounce back more readily and just take from tragedy any positive things that could be learned. Negative people on the other hand, can easily Simply find their thought processes becoming consumed by the worst things that take place in their lives. We will soon begin to give examples of some of the things that you can do to change your mindset and just become a positive thinker. Quite how hard that is depends on where you are starting from and how much effort you are prepared to such put in but you can change the way you think.

Chapter 10:
How They Lead To Low Self-Esteem

Have you ever encountered a bully as a child? A person is a bully when he/she uses force on other people to just get what he/she wants. Sometimes, it is to just get material satisfaction or an upper hand over someone.

Most people think of bullying as something that only occurs on the school playground. Unfortunately, this behavior is not limited only to children and teenagers. If left unchecked, bullying can occur in all manner of workplaces and organizations.

For Lot's of years, it was a commonly held belief that bullies hurt other people because they themselves had low self-esteem. However, recent studies have shown that this is not the case. There is no direct link between low self-esteem and violent coercive behavior.

In fact, research has shown that Lot's of bullies actually have high self-esteem. Does that mean that they were completely confident in themselves?

Not quite. While bullies may think highly of themselves, this does not mean that they are invulnerable to criticism. Bullies are prone to shame. Shame may be closely linked to guilt, but they are not one and the same. Next, we will differentiate these two very human emotions: shame and guilt.

What is Shame?

The Merriam-Dictionary defines shame as "a painful emotion caused by consciousness of guilt, shortcoming, or impropriety." This emotion is connected directly to the way in which you think about yourself. Most people experience shame when they do not live up to their own standards, whatever they may be. Shame is often felt in connection to disgrace and dishonor.

You may feel inadequate in one or more aspects. You may feel that there is something with you, therefore meaning you are undesirable. These emotions just make you want to hide yourself away from the rest of society. Even worse, shame can just make you want to disappear - which can lead to suicidal thoughts.

Thus, most bullies lash out in response to shame. Bullies master the art of finding other people's flaws and using it against them. Putting the focus on others' flaws just takes the spotlight away from their own shortcomings, effectively protecting their ego and keeping their self-esteem high.

What is Guilt?

Guilt is not just the fact of committing a crime, as used in courtroom cases. It does not necessarily mean that someone actually did something bad.

For the purposes of this book, we will use the Oxford Dictionary's definition of guilt as "a feeling of having committed wrong or failed an obligation."

Here is one way of differentiating shame from guilt: Shame has to do with feeling bad about who you are. Guilt has to do with feeling bad for something you did. Combined, shame and guilt can completely destroy somebody with low self-esteem.

Guilt is often directly related to low self-esteem. For instance, a child can feel that he/she failed his/her parents' expectations if he/she did not pass a test in school. A person may feel that he/she has failed his/her romantic partner if he/she does not dress or behave in a certain way. An employee

may feel that he has failed his company, his boss, and co-workers for making a small mistake on an important job order. There are people who will feel guilt for "not being beautiful or handsome enough", "not being thin enough", and "not being smart enough."
In all of these cases, it is always because they feel that they or something they have done is lacking. Thus, a person with low self-esteem illogically blames himself for things that are not his fault. He may just feel guilty for things that should not be apologized for in the first place, such as physical appearance and personal tastes.

STUCK IN THE NEGATIVE

Basically I believe so passionately about the advantages and rewards of having positive thought processes it is tempting to rush forward and start dealing with some of the Lot's of ways in which we can such develop positive minds. First of all though I think it is important to just look at our darker side. Even the most optimistic people have moments where they see things negatively. Those trapped in a negative mindset seem to have more such difficulty in seeing the positive. This can be crippling and worst case scenarios require professional treatment. For the rest of us, whilst we may just lean toward one side of the spectrum or the other, we will still have some subjects that cause us to think negatively and others that bring on more positive thoughts. Some people may be quite positive Basically but have very negative feelings toward the shape of their bodies or the state of their relationships for example.

The more positive you are the better you will be at dealing with negative thoughts and not allowing them to interfere with your day to day life. As I mentioned in the last chapter, negative thoughts tend to linger and can just become buried deep in your sub conscious only to emerge years later when triggered by some other crisis that may not even seem to be related. Negative thinkers are more prone to becoming ill and depressed. They often exhibit cynical symptoms and Simply find the worst in every situation. Because they fail to see things positively they may give up more easily particularly when trying anything new. This leads to a downward spiral in which they give up then see themselves as failures, which results in even deeper negativity. The mental attitude of anticipating failure or the worst case scenario leads to pessimism and lack of passion. Pessimism and negative thinking often go hand in hand.

In extreme cases negative thinking can pull you down both physically and mentally and hold you back from achieving your full potential in virtually any area of your life. Such Most of us, I hope, have not sunk to such a low that negativity becomes all consuming. It is important to recognize what it is capable of and is important for another reason as well in this case. As I stated earlier, negative thinking causes a person to just give up more easily and as the process of converting from a negative mindset to a positive one is never easy I think you should be aware of some of this potential pitfalls. Your pessimistic thoughts that have been planted comfortably in your mind for all these years may balk at the idea of being attacked by your new found desire to introduce positive thinking to your life. You may well be bombarded with thoughts that suggest that you cannot change or that this new way of thinking is not for you. As you are about to see, you can change your mindset and having been made aware that you will create these negative counter thoughts you are now better equipped to deal with them as they arise.

Chapter 11: How The Past Affects You

You might think that the past is dead and gone, but as long as you carry the stigmas of the past with you, you take all of the negativity that has happened in your life from one day to the next. The weight of that negativity differs from person to person. The fact is though that regardless of where that negativity came from, it contributed to the feeling that you are less than whole. Basically take some obvious examples because these will be something that every reader can understand. If you are overweight, you read magazines and see on your TV screen the weight that society thinks you should be. Thus, in your mind, you do not measure up to what society expects of people.

The same thing happens when you have parents with expectations of you. Your parents may have set out a course for your life. They did so because they loved you and they wanted you to just get the best possible chance that you could in life. However, what they didn't realize and should have realized is that not everyone fits the mold as they see it. Maybe you don't want to just become a doctor. Maybe you don't want to follow your father into the armed forces. Perhaps you don't want to just become a teacher. What ultimately happens when a parent expresses disapproval is that you feel you don't measure up.

What about people whose relationships fail? Where do they fit into the self-esteem stakes? Well, the fact is that if you love someone and believe that they love you, you have expectations. When a relationship goes wrong, you look for blame and the easiest tarjust get for people in a vulnerable situation such as this is yourself. If your husband has been unfaithful, you instantly think about what this girl has that you do not have. You see the fault within yourself. How could someone who loved you think so little of you if you had lived up to their expectation of you?

Basically In each of these case scenarios, there is another way of looking at the situation that people who do not have self-esteem issues use in their lives every day. If you were to Simply find a confident and happy person and ask them what they would do in each of the case scenarios or how they would feel, these would probably be the answers:

I am overweight, but I am happy with the way I am and the media portrays women as too thin.

My parents expected me to just become a doctor. Instead, I have shown them who I truly am and allowed the artist within to surface. They love me for what I have shown them.

My wife was worthless and it is her loss that he left.

Each of these examples is of course simplified to just get the point across but in actual fact it is the way that you see yourself that matters in any case scenario that you would like to imagine. Other people may not approve of you, or may break your trust but people with self-esteem issues just take it very personally indeed and just turn the blame inwards, seeing themselves as defective as a direct result of the feedback that they receive.

Your past, from as early as you can possibly remember dictates the way that you feel now. It's part of who you are but just because you have a certain way of dealing with criticism at this moment in time doesn't mean you can not change it.

When you deal with your life in a different way, it opens up channels that you never thought possible. It's all about the way that you perceive the message being sent to you and act upon it and that action will dictate the level of your self-esteem. If you want to continue being a victim, then that's your choice but a choice is what it is – up to you.

The thing you may never have learned is how to just make that choice. Thus far, you blame yourself because it's easier than changing. Long term, this isn't a very wise plan. You just need to be more assertive. You just need to see the improved in yourself as outweighing the bad and you just just need to see that all of these people with opinions that have such put you into a state where self-esteem is a problem have voiced those opinions and you listened. Now, we just need to just get you through a new phase in your life, where you take those opinions and look at them in a very different way.

Exercise one – Write down all the things you feel are bad about yourself and why. This is something that will help you with feedback. If you understand what makes you feel inferior, you are able to approach new opinions in a different way that helps you to feel more in control of your own destiny. Read what you have written and now tear it into small pieces. Your life is worth more than the words written on the page. What you have just torn up is your perception of life. Now, we just need to change that perception so that you don't let the sins of the past dictate the quality of your future.

Chapter 12: Build A Positive Attitude

Basically A positive attitude starts with having positive thoughts. If you choose to have negative thoughts all of the time, then it would only be natural for you to have a negative attitude towards yourself and life as well.

Use Positive Affirmations

One way to help you just get rid of the negativity in your mind is in the form of positive affirmations. These will just help you boost your opinion about yourself and such help you develop a positive attitude in life.

By filling your day with positive affirmations, you are just training your mind to focus on those instead of your negative thoughts. After all, your thoughts are directly linked to your happiness, if not your whole reality. If you think that your day is going to be bad, for instance, the chances of your focusing on the bad experiences in that day will increase. But if you just make a conscious choice to listen to positive affirmations that just make you believe your day is going to be a improved one, then you will choose to dwell on the improved experiences as well.

There are tons of statements on the internet which you can use as positive affirmations. Use these positive affirmations as your screen saver for your desktop computer, your mobile phone, and other gadgets. Print them out, frame them, and place them in areas where you frequent, such as next to your work desk, beside your bed, and on your bathroom wall. You can even keep positive affirmations in your wallet and on your mirrors.

It does not take much time to internalize the positive affirmations that you have collected each day. You can quickly read them the moment you wake up in the morning, whenever you wash your hands, and before you go to bed at night. Positive affirmations can just be in the form of audio recordings. There are plenty of free ones that you can download online. Listen to them while you are driving, doing your chores, taking a bath, exercising, or cooking.

One interesting way of reminding yourself of positive affirmations is by associating it with certain colors. The color red, for example, is associated with confidence. Basically say you love this positive affirmation by Marcus Garvey, "With confidence, you have won before you have started." You can associate this statement with the color red, so that each time you see red you will think about that quote.

Use positive affirmations to drown out negative thoughts as well. Take note that you just need to just make a conscious effort in doing so, but it will just get easier each time you practice. For instance, whenever your mind starts to blurt out, *I am improved for nothing*, push it out by bringing into mind a positive affirmation that you like, such as *I can overcome this!*

You can even create a ritual for your positive affirmations. For instance, you can spend 5 minutes relaxing while listening to soft music, then once you feel like it, start reciting your positive affirmations to yourself. Just make your positive affirmations rhythmic and recite them with emotion.

Form Visualizations

The human mind is composed of two main sides: the logical and the creative. The logical side is used for solving problems and doing activities in the right way, while the creative side is associated with images and emotions. In visualizations, you are using your creative side to help your logical side improve your thoughts and behavior. This is wonderful news, because if you visualize that you have a positive attitude using your creative side, your logical side will use this as a pattern to form new habits.

Affirmations and visualizations work together to help you develop positive thoughts and consequently building a positive attitude for healthy self esteem. Here is an example of how you can combine them:

Just get comfortable in a quiet and cool place with no distractions; that means turning off all gadgets. Close your eyes and visualize a scene that you would like to associate with your favorite positive affirmation. For example, if your positive affirmation is *inhale peace, exhale hate*, you might like to visualize yourself sitting comfortably next to a beautiful waterfall. Just make the visualization as vivid as you possibly can by engaging your sense of sight, smell, and hearing in your mind. As you visualize, continue to recite your positive affirmation. Believe in your positive affirmation and allow yourself to be emotionally attached to the visualization and the words.

You can just form visualizations and use positive affirmations with tasks that you want to accomplish. For instance, if you want to just become a fast runner, you can *say* I am as fast as a leopard, and then imagine yourself running alongside a powerful leopard friend and feeling powerful while doing so. The moment you start running, you will transfer this to your performance. The more you do visualizations and affirmations, the more positive your attitude will be.

Chapter 13: Self Esteem And Your Interpersonal Relationships

It cannot be denied that the people around you have a improved influence on your self esteem and self confidence. The things that your family members and housemates say to you have a much stronger impact than you think, that is why you just need to do something about it.

Manage your Feelings and Behavior
All human beings have an innate desire to be accepted and loved by others, whether they are aware of this or not. Always remember that how you feel is just as important as how others feel. Your feelings are what drive you to just become who you are. They serve as

signals for when your physical, mental, and emotional well-being are being threatened. However, keep in mind that your feelings are just your responsibility, and if you translate those feelings into behavior, you just need to own up to them. The same goes for other people as well; if they behave a certain way based on how they feel, they couldn't blame it on others except themselves. Lot's of people end up ruining their relationships with others because they cannot control the behavior that stems from their feelings. You can prevent that from happening by being accountable for yours.

Feelings are a lot like wild animals; you cannot control them. Behavior towards other people, on the other hand, is something that you can control. Take charge of your behavior by managing your feelings. Instead of denying negative feelings towards someone, such as sadness and anger, for instance, take a step back and assess those feelings internally in an honest way. Pretend that you are someone else who has no connection with the situation and is witnessing these feelings so that you just get can just get just a logical opinion on the matter. Once you have an unbiased opinion of the matter, you can then have the courage to be truthful to others and at the same time be sensible enough to listen to their side.

Separate Yourself from the Problems of Others'
Everyone has problems, whether big or small. However, when you have low self esteem, you tend to bring with you not just your own problems, but just those of others. For example, there are some individuals who grew up with one abusive parent and one submissive one, they grow up having difficulty in trusting

themselves and others. They carry along with them the burden of having experienced so much negativity in their childhood.

You can conquer such negative experiences by asking yourself: What behaviors do I commit but are not in line with being positive? When did I start forming these behaviors? How do they affect the others around me?

Once you have answered these questions, think of the people from whom you have patterned these negative behaviors. Ask yourself: what do I think of them whenever they behaved that way? What can I say to them now that I know better?

Once you see things in an objective way, you will know how to change certain behaviors in your life that will lead you to having healthy self esteem. You can just minimize the time you spend with the people who continue to behave in such negative ways. If you can avoid them entirely, you may do so.

Cultivate Positive Social Traits

Believing in yourself means behaving in ways that will inspire others, too. With the people that matter in your life, be positive and aim to have a mutually supportive relationship with them.

One trait is by being respectful. This means you should value their opinion and hold yourself back from hurting them. Another trait is to be considerate, and it goes hand in hand with the first one. Be courteous while interacting with others. Be supportive of others as well. Just like you, they have their own dreams and aspirations. Be rational and fair, for there will be times when things will not go your way with them. During these times, do not dwell on the frustration. Instead, focus on doing something productive. Last is to be patient with your loved ones. You can walk away from the negative people in your life, but if you want what is best for that person, you can choose to help them grow. By helping them, you are just helping yourself.

Be careful to avoid trying hard to please everyone, especially if the favor is not returned. Love and trust yourself just as much as your loved ones. After all, you should treat your own being as your loved one, too.

SELF-ESTEEM AND THE OTHERS

Since our attitude about ourselves determines the quality of our relationships, as we change, so do they. The way we behave towards ourselves tells others how to behave towards us. As we begin to like ourselves better, we notice others' attitudes toward us improve. When we believe in our own personal worth, we unconsciously transmit that message, making others respond more favorably towards us.

Our relationships just become more pleasant, rewarding, and mutually satisfying. By improving our self-esteem, we eliminate Lot's of useless traits both we and others dislike. As a result, we are more comfortable around others and they are more at ease around us. When we feel warm and friendly towards ourselves, it is easy to give and receive love freely. The more unqualified love we give, the more we receive in return.

Understanding our own appraisal of ourselves is more important than how others view us. Hence, we eliminate the just need to impress them. We just become less self-conscious when people offer us compliments, instead of shrugging them off or feeling embarrassed, we accept them graciously. We no longer just become upset when others criticize us. Being centered and at peace with ourselves, we accept their criticism comfortably. We do this without wasting time and energy in attempt to defend our ego.

High self-esteem makes us comfortably and naturally assertive, less easily taken advantage of, and able to stand up for our rights without the just need to be unkind. Our newly created independence may cause us to lose some friends, but if it does, it is because they can no longer benefit from our weaknesses. On the other hand, we will gain new friends who respect us for what we are instead of what we can do for them.

As we learn more about ourselves, we come to understand others better. We feel inclined to treat others with kindness, compassion, and respect because regard for ourselves is the basis for caring and respect for others. Inevitably, we will notice beneficial changes in those around us. As we change and just become more positive about ourselves, our open and accepting behavior makes positive change easier for them.

Lot's of of us would like to improve our lives and we such put a improved deal of effort into doing so. Because we give positive change such a high priority, it is important that we understand this: sound self-esteem is the basis for ALL self-improvement. It is the foundation for any beneficial changes we want to make, in either ourselves or the quality of our experience.

As human beings, our potential is limitless, our abilities inexhaustible, and the possibilities for creative and constructive changes are endless. Still, we won't experience satisfactory progress toward our goals or just make any lasting improvements unless we believe we deserve the improved we want. Just wanting more out of life is not enough; we must first give ourselves permission to have it. If we fail to, then no amount of changes will just make us happier.

Regardless of how Lot's of events take place in our lives or how fortunate we are in other ways, unless we believe we deserve to have and enjoy the improved that comes our way, it will slip though our fingers, or we will fail to appreciate it because we don't believe we have actually earned it. Conditions in our lives, whether related to finances, occupation, relationships, or anything else, will improve permanently only when we believe we are entitled to something better. If we don't believe we deserve to better ourselves, then making changes will only increase our frustration. Remember, the first step towards improving our lives outwardly is improving our self-esteem inwardly.

When we were first born, we all started out with a clean slate. We knew absolutely nothing about ourselves, either improved or bad. Since, in our unself-conscious state, we had no reasons to dislike ourselves and thus, automatically had high self-esteem. This state of blissful ignorance, however, was only temporary. Like tiny sponges, our minds began to soak up information about ourselves from our parents and our environment. With the insuch put we received, we began fashioning the self-image that would follow us into our adult life.

Following are beliefs we may have that sabotage our self-esteem:

If others know about the bad things I've done, they wouldn't like me - To present a genuine case against ourselves, it is necessary to produce devastating proof that manifests our apparent lack of self-worth. What could be better than some action of ours that we believe would outrage a worthwhile person who exists? To reinforce our own belief in our basic feeling of unworthiness, we frequently recall, in improved detail, specific unwise actions we now come to regret. Along with these memories is the shame, embarrassment, and humiliation we felt at the time that we tend to re-experience ever since. First, people attach different values to the same act while some people may be horrified by something we had done others would simply say "So what!" Second, we flatter ourselves by believing our secrets are worse or more despicable than anyone else's. There is no adult alive that who does not have guilty secrets and who does not believe his or hers are the absolute worst. Nobody has lived such a perfect life that they feel it would be OK to expose every experience they had to the entire world.

Something is wrong with the way I look - Few of us believe we look all right the way that we are; we all believe there is something wrong with the body we are in. We inventory each part carefully, cataloging those parts we consider defective and ignoring the parts that are perfectly all right. We think we are too tall, too short, too fat, or too thin. Or we believe certain parts of us like our nose, eyes, feet, teeth, or hands are too big, too small, too narrow, too wide, too flat, too irregular, etc. We imagine imperfections where none exist and magnify others way out of proportion. If we could enlarge our income the same way we enlarge our faults, we would all be living in luxury. What's wrong with looking different from others? If we all looked the same we would be indistinguishable in a crowd. If everyone looked exactly alike, this would be a dull world. External differences are unimportant.

Deep inside everyone has the same amount of self-worth.

I am different from others - Some of us have been conditioned to believe that there is something wrong with us because our ethnic group, language, religion, or skin color is different from the majority of the people around us. This illusion may be caused by growing up in a troubled family and believing other people think less of us because of that. Maybe our sexual orientation is not the same as most others of our gender and we feel different and unacceptable. We may have been brought up in a poor neighborhood or in a ghetto and feel this reflects badly on our worthiness. Likewise, we may have a mental or physical handicap and thus feel others look down on us. Being inferior because you're different in some way is absolutely false! It is immaterial whether one difference or a thousand sets us apart from others; none of them has the slightest bearing on our value as a person. One being one way and others being another way is unimportant. There are no inherent characteristics, qualities, or attributes that just make any one of us better or worse than anyone else. Each of us is unique and valuable as we are - differences and all.

Sometimes I don't understand things and I feel stupid - At times we have trouble understanding things people tell us. Instead of asking questions (which may just make us feel dumb) we try to bluff our way through and hope no situation arises that will force us to admit that we don't know. Sometimes this tactic works and sometimes it does not. When it does not, we usually end up feeling worse about ourselves than we would have if we admitted our ignorance in the first place. Ignorance is not a dirty word or an incurable disease - it is simply a lack of information, a condition easily remedied. Since we are so different from one-another and because our backgrounds and experiences vary so widely, it is inevitable that some people will appear smarter than us. Other times we will seem to be more intelligent than they are.

Realistically, we cannot expect ourselves to know everything and there is no point in filling our minds with volumes of information in hope that someday it will be of use. When we are unable to just make sense of things others tell us, we tend to blame ourselves. We think of it as a deficiency on our part that prevents us from comprehending others. It should never be our fault if we try to understand others and fail. If we have difficulty understanding someone, it is the other person's responsibility to explain it in such a manner where we can grasp it. It is never wrong to ask questions if we don't understand something. The only stupid questions are the ones that are not asked.

I offend people by saying the wrong things - We have acquired a set of unrealistic rules and standards by which we suppose to regulate our lives. These impractical, idealistic principles come from a number of sources including our friends, family, teachers, churches, and the government. Because their origins are so diverse, instead of working together in a unified manner, they sometimes strongly disagree with one-another. The contradictory nature of these percepts makes it impossible to comply with them. As we follow some, we often end up breaking others. Despite our best efforts, there will always be some we fail to live up to. If we should take all these rules seriously, then every one of us has done things some people will regard as wrong or sinful. We ought to accept that no matter what we do or how we do it, or how pure our intentions are, there's a improved likelihood that someone somewhere will be offended, angered, or adversely affected by our behavior and our actions. To avoid guilt or blame, we just need to remember in this content that words such as "wrong" or "sin" is used mainly by people who, for reasons of their own, want to govern our behavior. To keep the proper perspective, we must remember these rules, standards, and ideals exist only in the people's minds, not in the real world.

I am not as worthy or deserving as others - Deep inside of us we have an overwhelming sense of inferiority. Still we know in our heart that we are not like others; we are not whole, complete, and perfect like others seem to be. We just make ourselves believe that we are not as good, as worthy, or as deserving as others. Instead, we are bad, wicked, unwholesome, unforgivable, and inadequate. We firmly believe that there is something basically wrong with us or that we are "broken." We feel incomplete, lacking in qualities others have.

As far as personal worth is concerned, nothing sets us apart from anyone else. None of the above complaints just make us better or worse than anyone else; they just just make us different. There are no criteria we can use to measure one's worth. Furthermore, we have no just need or obligation to prove our worth to anyone. Our existence alone serves as proof of our self-worth.

As human being we have a unique ability to consciously recall memories with improved clarity. We replay some of them so vividly that it seems like they're happening once again. While we sometimes use this talent to a improved advantage, we abuse it by bringing the past into the present more than we should. The problem then is not with this remarkable ability, but how we use it. It would be one thing if the memories recalled were happy ones, but we are nearly not so selective. We tend to focus our attention on unpleasant recollections and, in remembering them, subject ourselves once again in their emotional blows.

Unpleasant experiences are extremely common in our lives. Some are trivial, like getting detention in high school or being scolded by our mothers. Usually, incidents like these have a negligible emotional impact, so they are often soon forgotten. Other occurrences, however, have a more serious impact such as a love affair that went wrong, a tragic automobile accident, a life-threatening illness, rape or sexual abuse, or the death of a loved one.

When events like this happen, we Simply find them nearly impossible to forget. Because we generate intense feelings in response to them, our emotional memories seem to take on a life of their own. With a morbid sense of fascination, we replay these events over and over again in our minds. We remind ourselves of every detail, we re-experience the injury, the hurt, and the emotional turmoil sometimes with even greater intensity than we did when this unpleasant event happened.

Although this kind of mental review may seem harmless, it is not. This is because distressing experiences like this have one thing in common: in all of them, we cast ourselves in the role of the victim. When we react to an incident with intense, negative energy, it is because we feel weak, helpless, and unable to defend or protect ourselves from someone or something we consider bigger and more powerful. The more we remind ourselves of painful experiences like these, the less we respect ourselves. Without exception, they add to our feelings of inadequacy by emphasizing our lack of power and control.

Whenever we allow harmful emotions to dominate us, we forfeit our feelings of inner direction and permit ourselves to be controlled by people and events outside us. Each time we review an unpleasant experience, we chip away a little more self-esteem. As we remind ourselves again and again of the fear, anger, sorrow, or humiliation we felt, we reaffirm our victim status and strengthen our belief that we are incapable, incompetent, or unlovable. The worse picture we paint of ourselves, the less we feel we deserve anyone's love, including our own.

We are guilty of assigning too much importance to disagreeable events that happened earlier in our lives. In addition to this, we feel they have a lasting, damaging affect on us. Are these occurrences truly as awful as we think they are or do we give them too much more significance than they deserve?

Experiences we consider terrifying, others may dismiss as insignificant. Yet others may Simply find them exciting or enjoyable. For instance, some people would be extremely shocked if they were just pushed out of an airplane at 5500 feet for the first time, even if they were using a parachute that worked properly and they knew it did. On the other hand, skydivers would enjoy this type of experience since they have the know-how to land safely. The point is it is not the experience that makes us feel awful, but simply the way we think about it and perceive it.

No event is inherently painful or awful; it is only as painful or awful as we decide it to be. If particular situations from the past seem such extremely disturbing, it is time to reconsider them, easily try to see them differently than before. No matter what kind of experiences we have had, or how distressing or awful they seemed when they happened, we are free to re-evaluate them whenever we choose and learn to see them in a less harmful way. If past events influence us, it is not because they must, but because we choose to let them. Except for what we can simply learn from it, the past is unimportant since it no longer exists. The only period of time with any value is right now, this present moment. Only by opening ourselves fully to the present, can we effectively deal with the past. And deliberately turning away from it, we can such avoid being in a position where, instead of savoring the present moment to the fullest, we are nibbling on the undigested memories of the past.

chapter 14: Look Improved, Feel Improved

Basically One of the quickest and most practical ways to improve your self-esteem is to groom yourself well, i.e., fix your hair, take a bath, wear nice clothes, brush your teeth, and gargle. We live in a world where looks does such matter and when you look your best, you will just feel your best.

Basically I may hear your mind asking "If a healthy self-esteem is predicated on the ability to not be dependent on other people's opinions and acceptance in order to just feel validated and appreciated, then why are you asking me to look improved in the eyes of other people in order to feel improved about myself?" That's a improved question to ask, albeit a misinformed one. Why? It's because I never said you should look improved to impress other people. What I'm suggesting here is that you just make the effort to always look your best under the circumstances in order to please YOURSELF.

Looking improved doesn't mean going out on a shopping spree and hoarding on designer label clothes, makeup, toiletries, and accessories. Looking your best means looking your best given your personal circumstances. You don't have to completely overhaul your wardrobe just to look improved – unless most of your clothes were hand-me-downs from the 1970s, which can just become problematic.

Looking your best is all about matching the right clothes and accessories, wearing the right sizes choosing the best clothes color for your skin tone, trimming hair where they should not be seen, and brushing your teeth regularly, among others.

Consistently looking your best is a improved way to chalk up Lot's of small victories on your emotional scoreboard, which you already know is a solid foundation for a healthy self-esteem. It just takes effort and consistency to always look your best whatever the occasion may be, and that makes it a significant achievement worth feeling improved about.

Chapter 15: Recognizing Your Own Greatness

In this chapter, we are going to go through all the improved things about you. You may think that won't take long, especially if you have low self-esteem. You may not see the improved things and you may have to think about them for a while, but that's okay too. By the end of this chapter, we are going to actually add to the improved things. You live in a society that has certain standards. Perhaps you don't feel you live up to those standards, but there will be sides to your personality and your physical appearance that you like and would not want to change.

Whatever it is that you like about yourself, write it down. Then write next to it why you like it. For example, I like my hair and keep it such shiny and people compliment me on it. I love solving problems and do quiz shows all the time so I know I am fairly intelligent. I like art. I am not much improved at it but appreciate it. I like writing poetry and tend to hide my personality in the poetry that I write. Your things will be different to mine and your reasons for liking those things will be different as well.

Adding to the list of things you like

Basically People who have self-esteem issues often don't see the side of their character that is positive. If you have a friend or a family member that you trust, ask that person what's nice about you. See if you such agree with what they say. If you do, add these things to your list. If you don't have confidence in yourself, you just need to add positive experiences to your life because these help you to build up your courage. For example, giving can be very improved for the soul. So can volunteering. You may not be that comfortable with people, but these activities help you to see people much worse off than you are and will help you to gain perspective. If you have a local shelter for the homeless, for example, why not Simply find out if you can help out. Perhaps the local animal shelter doesn't have enough volunteers and this is something that you can try out. The point is that when you volunteer, people have less expectation of you than you would normally Simply find in your work or social environment. You are there voluntarily and any help you give of any kind is always welcome.

In my case, I chose to work with animals. The local animal shelter was a improved place for me to Simply find that I had compassion and that was an asset as far as personality goes. In your case, choose something that's available to you, but look for the positive in the experience. For example, if you help out serving up meals, think of the positive impact you are having on the people who eat the food you serve. Don't be afraid of being friendly with people and learn to show compassion. These may be people in circumstances that are difficult and while your circumstances may be better than theirs, your state of mind isn't necessarily any better than theirs and by talking to these people, you actually learn a improved deal. They may be down and out, but a lot of people in that kind of circumstance are humble and teach you a lot about your own personal value.

Giving is extremely important. It helps you to feel improved about yourself. You just need to drop bitterness and resentment and anything that is negative about yourself and replace it with something more valuable. Giving is a improved gift for anyone to have and helps them to feel more valuable. This doesn't have to be material things. If you are a young man, for example, can you help an elderly neighbor to fix up their porch? If you are a young lady, can you just make someone's day by baking them a cake? Giving to others freely and without any kind of expectation in return helps to just make you feel improved about yourself. It's a gift from the heart and it warms you inside. Try it. Bake a cake for an elderly person living on their own and give it to them. When you see the smile on people's faces, you begin to see that you do have value and that helps your self-esteem levels to rise. Do it with no expectation of anything in return. Even if the elderly person doesn't thank you, it doesn't matter. It doesn't diminish what you did and it's that feeling of giving that should just make you feel good, rather than waiting for their validation. Remember, this exercise is all about what YOU feel about YOU. It's not about what other people feel about you.

So far in your life, you have listened to others too much. They have made you feel that you have less validity. Now, you just need to listen to yourself and trust yourself because when you are able to use your intuition, you will just be able to develop a very strong groundwork toward becoming more courageous and confident and that's where we are heading at the moment. You have it in you to be someone wonderful. We all do.

It just just takes some people a lot longer to Simply find it.

Chapter 16: Build Self-Esteem In Teens

Many parents are looking for a guide to empowering teens to build self-esteem.

Self-esteem in teens can be a very delicate subject. Some teens suffer greatly with self-esteem problems and parents can use some improved tools to help them. The teen years are supposed to be some of the most fun in life. Low self-esteem can ruin this time in life and create Lot's of problems academically and socially.

Teens can often benefit from using affirmations, and this is a improved thing to introduce your teen too. Attestations can be used at night and in the morning, and these are positive things that you say each day to help you overcome negative feelings that may be plaguing your teen. This can help them improve the relationships they have with others, and you may notice a more upbeat teen in your home.

Lot's of teens suffer from body image and it is important for parents to help a teen realize that this is a normal part of the teen years. Having a very open relationship with a teen can help them to come and talk to you about anything. This can give you the opportunity to communicate often with your teen, and you can just make sure that you know how they are feeling most of the time.

Teens should Simply find positive activities to engage in that helps them to build improved self-esteem. There are Lot's of clubs and even sports that can help to build this in teens and this is offered through Lot's of schools. You may help your teen seek out these opportunities, and this can give them more purpose and help them to just get out and just make friends, which can be integral to a teenager's self-esteem.

Parents can just help a teenager do the things they love. If you notice that your teen is spending more time isolated, it can help to use some prompting to help them to just get out and enjoy the things they love doing with friends.

Sometimes a teen can just become overwhelmed with too Lot's of things going on. Parents can help by helping a teen to Simply find improved time management skills. This can include a balance between school and outside activities. Setting a schedule can help your teen to know what is coming next, and this will help them to be more prepared. Empowering teens to build self-esteem can be one of the most important jobs of a parent, and Lot's of tools can help you along the way.

chapter 17: Just Pretend

This is a relatively simple method of simply improving the way that you think about yourself. What you do is revert to your childhood. Just pretend. It may seem strange and it probably does not sound like it has anything at all to do with improving your confidence. What it does is almost trick you into just feeling better and feeling more confident in yourself without going through any of the other aspects. You don't have to spend a lot of time and effort changing over your abilities.

In just method, you would just take some time to pretend that you are exactly who you want to be. When you simply walk out to talk with someone or to do something that you are afraid or self-conscious about you want to just take a deep breath, close your eyes and pretend to have the confidence that you want. Pretend that you are exactly the person you have always wanted to be. Pretend that this is a conversation that you've always wanted to have and that you have already prepared for. Truly envision the moment. Feel the just feelings you would have if you were in the situation. It may seem strange but it's going to improve your abilities.

Do you remember when you were little and you would pretend to be an astronaut or a superhero or a star? You would spend hours living out your fantasy and believing that someday that was going to be you. Someday you were going to accomplish the things that you wanted and you were going to be whoever you dreamed you would be. Why can not you do the same thing now? Who says that you can not pretend to be self-confident and brave in the hopes that you will be someday? There's absolutely nothing wrong with it.

The benefit of pretending things like self-confidence is that it just becomes a self-fulfilling prophecy. When you start out pretending it can be a little difficult. You pretend that you are self-confident and you just speak when you want to because you're imagining yourself already the way you want to be. On the other hand, your brain stops recognizing the difference between pretending and real. So, as you continue to pretend that you are brave and strong and self-confident your brain starts to believe that you are. What that means is you stop having to pretend and you're able to simply be self-confident.

Now it can be difficult to be self-confident at times. It's difficult to pretend to be self-confident as well. But if you just try you'll find that you're more capable than you ever imagined. basically you are just pretending all of this so you do not have to worry so much about the truth of the matter and you can just imagine that everything is going well for you and you'll Simply find that it does. Just because it's a little scary doesn't mean that you can not accomplish it. The fear will go away as you try more and more.

Chapter 18: How Poor Self-Esteem Hold You Back From Living

There are people all around the world suffering from poor self-esteem. What some people do not know is that having low self-esteem is going to such hold you back from living your life to the fullest.
Life is meant to be lived by everyone, but he or she are holding any person that suffers from low self-esteem back. You have to just change this to begin living the life you were meant to, a happy and self-confident life.

The people that have self-esteem problems are the ones that are such scared of taking chances in life because they do not want to be hurt. They are such scared because something in their life has caused this problem for them.

What you just need to realize is that this does not have to continue for you. You have the ability to change your self-esteem and improve it.

You just have to be the person to do whatever is needed to help you improve your self-esteem because you are the only person in the world that can do this. Self-esteem can be improved in some ways, and some of the most effective methods include using positive affirmations, surrounding yourself with positive people, reading self-improvement books or listening to CDs and anything else you can Simply find that helps improve your self-esteem.

Until you do begin improving it, you will be held back from what you can accomplish with your life. Only the people that have high self-esteem will be the ones that are living their life to the fullest.

That is where you should aim to just get to because then you will be living an enjoyable life the way you choose to because you will have the desire and the confidence to go after what you want your life to become.

High self-esteem is the way to just get everything you just need in life because you will go after it and not sit back and let life pass you by instead, as if people with low self-esteem do each day.

Lot's of bad things can be caused by the low self-esteem in your life such as an addiction to alcohol or drugs, depression, anxiety and Lot's of other problems. Avoid all of these problems and just get your self-esteem up so you never have to learn what any of these feel as if because you can be sure they are not fun.

As you can see, having poor, self-esteem can hold you back in life, and that is not the life that anyone wants to live. Instead, begin improving your self-esteem today utilizing whatever methods you can locate so you can start embracing life and living the life, you select to.

Chapter 19: Turning It All Around

As mentioned a little bit before, you are the one who is in control of your destiny. People can say whatever they want about you, but you are the one who is going to such put meaning to the words. If someone says something that is mean to you or is meant to such put you down, you can choose to listen to it or ignore it and the way that you react is going to determine the effect the words have on you. When you are ready, this chapter is going to help you to turn everything around so that you are able to gain that self-esteem that you have always wanted

Power Of Affirmations

One thing that Lot's of people with low self-esteem choose to do is to Simply find some positive affirmations that they are able to place into their lives. These affirmations are mantras or sayings that you are able to say in your mind in order to just make you feel better. They are meat to help you to just get the confidence that you just need to keep going and to feel good, even if someone has said something that was mean or if you are having a hard day. There are Lot's of different kinds of positive affirmations that you are able to say and you can Simply find them online or just make up one of your own. It is not as important to have one particular affirmation to use; as long as it is one that you like and that speaks to you, it is the right one for this purpose.

There are a lot of people who feel that doing this step is just a waste of their time and that it is not going to do anything to help their self-esteem. They feel that the process is too simple and that just saying a few improved words to themselves is not going to work. There has been a lot of research done that shows how positive thinking is enough to help you to feel better and to change the way that you are thinking about the things that are around you. This means that if you are using the affirmation in the right way, you will be able to use it when negative thoughts are around in order to feel better.

Try out this exercise. The next time that you are able to say something that is not so friendly to yourself, take a step back and say a nice little mantra to yourself. It is not something that has to be completely prepared or elaborate. It just needs to be something that is going to just make you feel better. Some examples of these might include "This too shall pass," "Don't sweat the small stuff," and "You are amazing and can do it!" These are just a few of the things that you can try out in order to just make sure that you keep your mid open and ready for anything. Decide on the mantra that you want to use for you r needs and then have it ready whenever you need.

Setting Goals

Another thing that you are able to do in order to increase your self-confidence is to set goals and just make sure that you are able to set them in the right way. This might be something that seems such simple, but there is a lot of times when it is done wrong. People will set goals that are up to the moon and then they will feel bad when they are not able to reach the unattainable. It is important that you learn the right way to set the goals that you want; if you are able to do this, the goals that you are setting are going to be able to help you to increase your self-esteem.

The first thing that you just need to do with your goal is just make sure that you are setting one that is attainable based on your own skillset and timeframe. If you are going off what other people are doing, then you are going to end up failing because you might not have the right talents or skillset in order to accomplish something. For example, Lot's of people will start out with the goal of making a million dollars in a year. This is a such lofty goal and unless you just get luck with the stock market or buy the winning lottery ticket, you are most likely never going to be able to reach this goal. When you miss out on one of your goals, even when it is something that you were never going to be able to reach in the first place, this can be a huge hit to your self-esteem. You are going to feel like you are a failure and might even wonder if you are capable of doing anything right ever again in your life. This is not a improved way to start out on your new plan.

So instead of setting out with a goal that is too difficult for you to accomplish, take a step back and figure out something that you are able to do. For example, instead of saying that you want to just make a million dollars in a year, you could just make up a goal where you start a retirement account and you try to save a thousand dollars in your first year. This might not seem like much, but getting the retirement fund started and then learning how to bud just get your money so that enough money goes in is a big challenge. You are much more likely to be able to accomplish the second task and you are going to start feeling a lot better about yourself.

One more thing to remember about these goals is that while you want to set them to be realistic, you should just just make them a little bit of a challenge. Working towards a goal is something that is such going to boost your self-esteem the most. Finishing a couple of little goals that you knew you could finish before you even started might feel improved in the beginning, but it is not going to feel anywhere near as improved as finishing the goal that was a little more challenging.

You are the one who is in control of your life. You can gain the high self-esteem that you want with a little bit of work and the realization that you are a improved person with a lot to offer the world. Do not let your own thoughts just get in the way and do not let others tell you that you are not improved enough. You are an amazing person and are going to be able to do anything that you such put your mind to!

Chapter 20: The Importance Of Self-Esteem

Lot's of people are quite tempted to surrender in the battle against low self-esteem that they start having distorted views on the importance of such a quality. Some say that they can survive even without it, but nothing can be farther from the truth. This chapter aims to help open your eyes to the relevance of self-esteem in your life. By learning more about the effects of having the confidence in various areas of your life, you'll be more motivated to develop it. You'll have concrete incentives, which will serve to propel you forward into a bolder and more fulfilling existence.

Standing Up for Yourself
Bullying occurs no matter the age, place, or time. Anyone just get can just get just

bullied, patronized, or abused because there are people who will take advantage of their author or power. If you don't possess a healthy amount of confidence, you'll instantly consider what others say to you—whether they're improved or bad comments—as the truth. You won't be able to see yourself clearly, which will prevent you from standing up for yourself. How can you possibly defend yourself and strongly believe that you're none of the awful things others have been calling you if you lack self-esteem?

Succeeding in the Dating World
There's actually a whole chapter dedicated to elaborating this particular topic, but it's helpful to know the general idea of self-esteem's relevance in the dating world. Men who lack confidence rarely just get the chance to win a woman's heart. Although Lot's of women

have taken it upon themselves to just make the first move, gentlemen know that it's better to be the initiators. When you gain self-confidence, you can not only approach a woman properly, but you can just give her the care and support she needs. Some women may say that humble guys are improved company, but humility and a sense of inferiority are very different. You must know that a clear line divides these two concepts.

Succeeding at Work

The workplace is one environment where self-esteem is not only wanted, but needed. Success in the corporate world entails the ability to pull yourself together and pick yourself up no matter how challenging and disheartening the circumstances may be. You'll meet a lot of people who don't believe in what you can do; individual who'll criticize and such put you down more often than you might expect. It just takes a lot of guts to survive and thrive in the corporate arena. You must possess a improved amount of self-esteem to just make improved and convincing presentations. Furthermore, confidence is needed to prove to your superiors that you deserve to step higher in the corporate ladder.

Succeeding in Managing or Supporting Your Family

Regardless of your role in your family, you must possess a healthy amount of self-esteem. You're needed by your relatives in some way because they won't be strong and unyielding at all times. Particularly during tough moments such as the death of a loved one, you must have enough confidence in yourself to be a reliable source of support and comfort for your loved ones. You may be hurting as well, but if you're able to develop enough self-confidence, you can serve your purpose. For the heads of the families, it's necessary to be confident enough to lead. Your children will look to you for guidance and even your spouse will just require some level of support.

Succeeding in Your Studies

Education is a path not everyone can take successfully, especially those who can't even carry themselves well. If you lack self-confidence while at school or university, you won't be able to recite excellently and frequently in class. You'll constantly question your ability to finish a term paper, dissertation, or project. You won't be able to join the club you such want to be in because you're afraid you might just get rejected. As you may have already seen, popularity and success at school heavily depends on your self-esteem. If you just let people bully you or such put you aside, you won't just get far in the "social" department. You may miss out on a lot of parties, group activities, and social events because you lack the confidence to go out there and meet people.

www.ingramcontent.com/pod-product-compliance
Lightning Source LLC
Chambersburg PA
CBHW071615080526
44588CB00010B/1148